PIANO

Adventures® *by Nancy and Randall Faber*

THE BASIC PIANO METHOD

CONTENTS

About the "Sightreading Stocking Stuffers"

A student's enthusiasm for learning Christmas music can become an opportunity to create enthusiasm for sightreading. In this book, each Christmas song is presented with short melodies, called "Sightreading Stocking Stuffers."

The "Sightreading Stocking Stuffers" are **melodic variations** of the carol being studied. Teachers will notice that the lyrics and rhythm patterns are from the carol. By drawing on these familiar rhythms, the student may effectively focus on interval reading and note reading.

The student should sightread one "stocking stuffer" a day while learning the Christmas song. Or, the stocking stuffers can be used as sightreading during the lesson itself.

The teacher may wish to tell the student:

> **Sightreading means "reading music at first sight."**
>
> When sightreading, music is not practiced over and over. Instead, it is only played once or twice with the highest concentration.

The following **3 C's** may help the student with sightreading:

 CORRECT HAND POSITION
Find the correct starting note for each hand.

 COUNT - OFF
Set a steady tempo by counting one "free" measure before starting to play.

 CONCENTRATE
Focus your eyes on the music, carefully watching for **steps** and **skips.**

FF1137

Note to Teacher: This page reviews beginning reading concepts and prepares the student for the carols and sightreading that follow.

Stuffing the Stockings

These musical "gifts" either **step**, **skip** or **repeat**. Draw a line connecting each "gift" to the correct stocking.

Extra Credit: Play each "gift" on the piano using the fingering given.

Jolly Old Saint Nicholas

Traditional

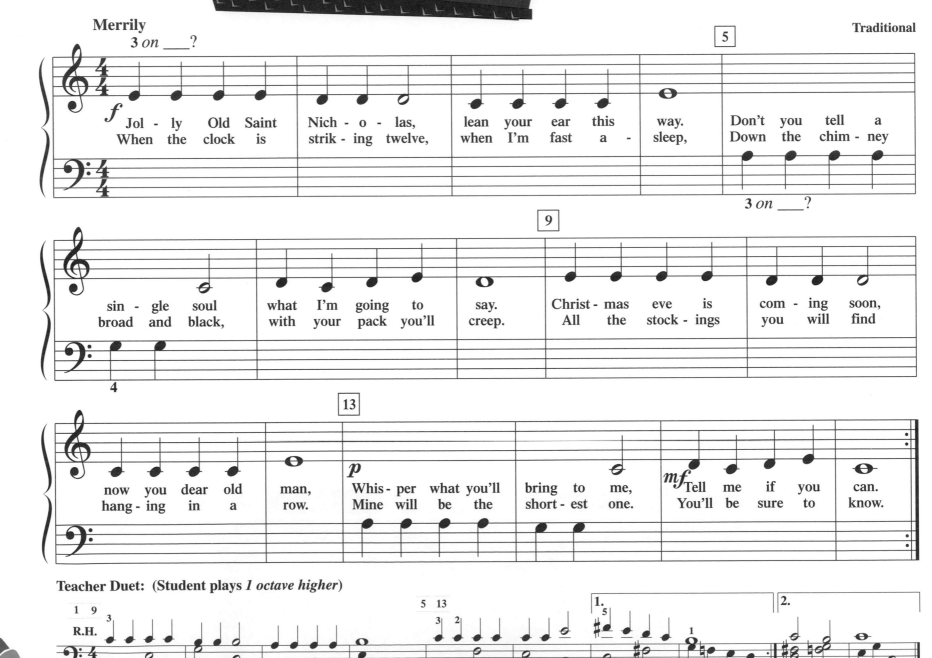

Merrily

3 *on* ___?

f

Jol - ly Old Saint | Nich - o - las, | lean your ear this | way. | Don't you tell a
When the clock is | strik - ing twelve, | when I'm fast a - | sleep. | Down the chim - ney

3 *on* ___?

sin - gle soul | what I'm going to | say. | Christ - mas eve is | com - ing soon,
broad and black, | with your pack you'll | creep. | All the stock - ings | you will find

now you dear old | man, | *p* Whis - per what you'll | bring to me, | *mf* Tell me if you | can.
hang - ing in a | row. | Mine will be the | short - est one. | You'll be sure to | know.

Teacher Duet: (Student plays *1 octave higher*)

R.H.

L.H.

mp *p* *mp* *mf* *mp*

1. **2.**

Repeat for 2nd verse

FF11?

Note: The words are familiar, but the **melodies have changed**.
The words will help you with the rhythm, but watch for steps and skips!

Sightread one "stocking stuffer" a day
while learning *Jolly Old Saint Nicholas*.

Circle the stocking after sightreading!

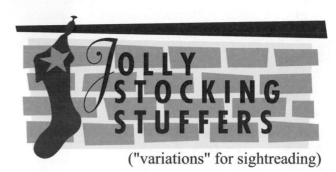

("variations" for sightreading)

DAY 1
3 *on* ___?
mf
(Jol - ly Old Saint Nich - o - las, lean your ear this way. *2 - 3 - 4*)

DAY 2
2 *on* ___?
mf
(Tell me if you can. *2 - 3 - 4* Tell me if you can! *2 - 3 - 4*)

DAY 3
L.H. (Whis - per what you'll bring to me. *mf* Tell me if you can. *2 - 3 - 4*)
p
3 *on* ___?

DAY 4
L.H. (Mine will be the short - est one. *mf* You'll be sure to know. *2 - 3 - 4*)
p
1 *on* ___?

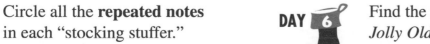

DAY 5 Circle all the **repeated notes**
in each "stocking stuffer."

DAY 6 Find the first 2 measures of **Day 2** "stocking stuffer" in
Jolly Old Saint Nicholas. Circle these 2 measures in the carol.

Now circle the last 2 measures of **Day 2** "stocking stuffer" in the carol.

Good King Wenceslas

Moderately

Traditional

repeat!

1 *on* ___?

mf
Good King Wen - ces - las looked out on the feast of Ste - phen.
When the snow lay 'round a - bout, deep and crisp and e - ven.

4 *on* ___?

9

f
Bright - ly shone the moon that night, though the frost was cru - el.
p

13

mf
When a poor man came in sight, gath - 'ring win - ter fu - el.

4

Teacher Duet: (Student plays *1 octave higher*)

R.H.
mp
L.H.

FF1137

Sightread one "stocking stuffer" a day
while learning *Good King Wenceslas.*

Circle the stocking after sightreading!

WINTER STOCKING STUFFERS

("variations" for sightreading)

DAY 1 — **1** *on* ___?

(Good King Wen - ces - las looked out. Good King Wen - ces - las looked out.)

DAY 2 — **5** *on* ___?

(Bright - ly shone the moon that night. Bright - ly shone the moon that night.)

DAY 3 — L.H. (Though the frost was cru - el. Though the frost was cruel.)

3 *on* ___?

DAY 4 — L.H. (When a poor man came in sight, gath - 'ring win - ter fuel.)

4 *on* ___?

DAY 5 — In the "stocking stuffers" above, put a ✔
above each measure with this rhythm.

DAY 6 — Find **measures 9-10** of *Good King Wenceslas* in one of the
"stocking stuffers" above.
Then circle these 2 measures in the "stocking stuffer".

Jingle Bells

Hint: The shaded boxes will help you with these measures.

Cheerfully

J. Pierpont

Teacher Duet: (Student plays *2 octaves higher*)

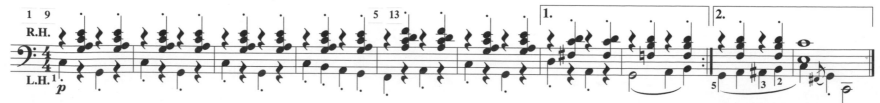

FF1137

Sightread one "stocking stuffer" a day while learning *Jingle Bells*.

Circle the stocking after sightreading!

("variations" for sightreading)

DAY 1
3 on ___?
𝆑 (Jin - gle bells, jin - gle bells, jin - gle all the way!)

DAY 2
5 on ___?
𝆑 (Jin - gle bells, jin - gle bells, jin - gle bells, jin - gle bells.)

DAY 3 L.H.
mf
(Oh, what fun it is to ride in (a) one - horse o - pen sleigh!)
5 on ___?

DAY 4 L.H.
mf
(Jin - gle bells, jin - gle bells, jin - gle all the way!)
1
5

DAY 5 In the "stocking stuffers" above, put a ✔ above each measure with this rhythm.

DAY 6 Write the letter name beside each note for **Day 3.**

Away in a Manger

Circle all the **repeated notes** before playing.

Words and Music by
J.E. Spilman and Martin Luther

Teacher Duet: (Student plays *1 octave higher*)

Repeat for 2nd verse   FF1137

Sightread one "stocking stuffer" a day
while learning *Away in a Manger.*

Circle the stocking after sightreading!

Hint: Repeated notes are circled to help you sightread.

CHRISTMAS STOCKING STUFFERS

("variations" for sightreading)

Go, Tell It on the Mountain

Sightread one "stocking stuffer" a day
while learning *Go, Tell It on the Mountain.*

Circle the stocking after sightreading!

JOLLY STOCKING STUFFERS

("variations" for sightreading)

DAY 1

3 *on* ___?

𝆑 (Go, *(2 - 3 - 4)* | tell it on the | moun - | tain.)

3 *on* ___?

DAY 2

1 *on* ___?

𝆑 (Go, *(2 - 3 - 4)* | tell it on the | moun - | tain.)

4 *on* ___?

DAY 3

2 *on* ___?

𝆑 (O - ver the | hills and | ev - 'ry - | where.__)

3 *on* ___?

DAY 4

5 *on* ___?

𝆑 (Je - sus | Christ__ is | born._____ |)

DAY 5
Circle all the LINE to LINE **skips** in
each "stocking stuffer." There are 7.

Hint: Don't forget to look over the barline!

DAY 6
Which "stocking stuffer" is exactly the same as
the music in *Go, Tell It on the Mountain*?

Day ____

We Wish You a Merry Christmas

Merrily

Traditional English

Teacher Duet: (Student plays *1 octave higher*)

(We wish you a Mer-ry Christ - mas, We wish you a Mer-ry Christ - mas, We wish you a Mer-ry Christ - mas and a Hap - py New Year!___)

14

FF1137

Sightread one "stocking stuffer" a day
while learning *We Wish You a Merry Christmas.*

Circle the stocking after sightreading!

MERRY STOCKING STUFFERS

("variations" for sightreading)

DAY 1

3 *on* ___?

f (We wish you a Mer - ry Christ - mas!)

DAY 2

1 *on* ___?

mf (We wish you a Mer - ry Christ - mas!)

DAY 3

L.H. (We wish you a Mer - ry Christ - mas!)

f

4 *on* ___?

DAY 4

L.H. (We wish you a Mer - ry Christ - mas!)

mf

1 *on* ___?

DAY 5

Circle all the skips in each "stocking stuffer" above.
Hint: There are 5.

DAY 6

Can you sing *We Wish You a Merry Christmas*
without playing the piano?

Christmas Music Calendar

Complete the music calendar for each day of December.

1 ♩ = ___ beat

2 Write the music alphabet: ___ ___ ___ ___ ___ ___ ___

3 𝅗𝅥 = ___ beats

4 In which clef would Mrs. Santa sing? *(circle)* 𝄢 or 𝄞

5 In which clef would Santa sing? *(circle)* 𝄢 or 𝄞

6 A staff has ___ lines.

7 A staff has ___ spaces.

8 𝅗𝅥. = ___ beats

9 How would Santa say, "Merry Christmas to all!" *p mf f*

10 Circle the whole notes.

11 Write the sign for **soft** sleigh bells. ___

12 Write the sign for **moderately loud** reindeer hooves. ___

13 4/4 means ___ beats in a measure.

14 A step UP from **D** (*Dasher*) is ___

15 3/4 means ___ beats in a measure.

16 A step DOWN from **B** (*Blitzen*) is ___

17 A skip UP from **D** (*Donner*) is ___

18 A skip DOWN from **C** (*Comet*) is ___

19 Circle the star on the **G** line.

20 Circle the star on the **F** line.

21 How many **C**'s (for "candy canes") are on the piano? ___

22 How many 2-black-key groups are on the piano? ___

23 How many 3-black-key groups are on the piano? ___

24 CHRISTMAS EVE! How many keys are on the piano? ___

25 CHRISTMAS DAY! Play your favorite Christmas songs!